ARMOR AT WAR SERIES

PANZERS IN THE EAST

(1) The Years of Aggression 1941-1943

CONCORD
PUBLICATIONS COMPANY

Editor: James Hill

Copyright © 1997

by CONCORD PUBLICATIONS CO.

603-609 Castle Peak Road

Kong Nam Industrial Building

10/F, B1, Tsuen Wan

New Territories, Hong Kong

We welcome authors who can help
expand our range of books. If you
would like to submit material,
please feel free to contract us.

We are always on the look-out for new,
unpublished photos for this series.
If you have photos or slides or
information you feel may be useful to
future volumes, please send them to us
for possible future publication.
Full photo credits will be given upon
publication.

ISBN 962-361-620-1

printed in Hong Kong

*All photos published in this book are from: Military
Institute of History, Central Military Archive, Military Photo
Agency and private collections of the following persons:
T. Kopanski, R. Bock, D. Maslov, and the author. I would
like to give thanks to these people and the crews of these
institutions for their help and patience.*

Introduction

The First Summer - 1941

In the autumn of 1940, following a series of regrettable political decisions, the world was plunged into a nearly global war, which was later named World War Two. None of the countries involved was really ready for the bloody slaughter. Nor did any of them have time to make necessary preparations. Of course, Germany's Third Reich faced this same predicament. The questionable decisions Hitler made in 1940 resulted in a German Army that was not strong enough and was equipped with outdated weapons.

Within Das Heer (the Army), this problem was the most extreme in the Panzerwaffe, the armored shock force of the land army. Without armored units, all of Das Heer's efforts would be useless. But these all-important divisions suffered from a lack of trucks, good tanks and other vehicles, as well as powerful anti-tank guns. For example, the production of tanks in 1940 was 1,600 vehicles, only 600 tanks more than in 1939. Even worse was that many of the tanks were old models.

The biggest problem, however, was the main armored personal carrier, the Sd.Kfz. 251, of which only 337 were produced. This was only 105 more than in the previous year! Each motorized infantry battalion in a Panzerdivision needed about 100 Hanomags. So, during the whole of 1940, Germany could arm only three out of about 80 battalions in about 20 armored divisions with these vehicles! Without this vehicle, a complete armored attack, typical of the Panzerwaffe's tactics on an open field, was almost impossible.

Nevertheless, the strength of the Panzerwaffe increased from 3,500 tanks in the beginning of May 1940 to 5,250 tanks in the beginning of June 1941, but only 3,332 of them could be put into action against the "Red" forces. This was the largest armored force created by any country in Europe, but it was a little too small to wage war against a new enemy.

The force contained 410 Pz.Kpfw. I and 746 Pz.Kpfw. II light tanks, so one-third of the entire tank force concentrated on the German-Soviet border (of which 230 were command tanks) was useless on a modern battlefield! There were also 623 Pz.Kpfw. 38(t)s and 149 Pz.Kpfw. 35(t)s. These were worse in some ways than the Pz.Kpfw. III, which was the standard German tank at the time. In all of the armored divisions, only 439 Pz.Kpfw. IVs were available, and this vehicle was the only capable and powerful tank in the Panzerwaffe.

However, even if the Pz.Kpfw. IV was the best German tank at this time, it could be strongly opposed by the Soviet T-34 and American M4 Sherman tanks. The German tanks had been produced up to 1937, while the Allied tanks were put into production in the 1940-1941 period. Thus, they were much more modern, which means they were better in many ways. Germany had nothing that could provide its own crews with superiority over the enemy. A balance could be achieved sometimes against the T-34, but it was very quickly lost when Soviet KV tanks went into action.

This problem - too small a number of tanks combined with the weaknesses inherent in them - is more recognizable when we compare these 3,332 tanks against the 17,000 Soviet tanks concentrated on the western border of the Soviet Union. Among them were 1,500 T-34 or KV-1 and KV-2 tanks. This "iron fist" could demolish the whole power of the Panzerwaffe on the eastern border of Germany almost instantly when properly and productively used.

The first German panzer attack force arrived at the German-Soviet border in September 1940, when the 2.Inf.Div.(mot.) and the 1., 5. and 6.Panzerdivisions were sent to General Gubernya after a Romanian-Hungarian-German agreement was reached. The next main force arrived between December 1940 and February 1941, when six rapid attack forces were sent to areas west of the Bug river. But the main part of the Panzerwaffe arrived at the Soviet border in May 1941 - six motorized and ten armored divisions. In all, on 22nd June 1941, there were 17 Panzerdivisions, 14 motorized infantry divisions (including four Waffen-SS) and five motorized brigades (including three Waffen-SS) ready. Apart from the tanks already mentioned, the following force was concentrated: 85 Flammpanzers in three battalions, 80 tracked tank destroyers in four battalions, 24 Flakpanzers in one battalion and 230 StuGs in eleven battalions and five batteries. There were also 36 sIGs and about 900 armored cars in divisions and about 500 (armored and non-armored) wheeled or tracked combat vehicles in divisions or independent anti-tank or anti-aircraft battalions.

The mechanized divisions and brigades were organized into Panzergruppen as follows:

Pz.Gr.1 -
III.Pz.Kp. - 13.Pz.Div., 14.Pz.Div., 25.Inf.Div.(mot.)
XIV.Pz.Kp. - 9.Pz.Div., 16.Pz.Div.,
        SS-Div.(mot.) 'Wiking'
XLVIII.Pz.Kp. - 11.Pz.Div., 16.Inf.Div.(mot.)
reserve - SS-Div.(mot.) 'LAH', 60.Inf.Div.(mot.)
Pz.Gr.2 -
XXIV.Pz.Kp. - 3.Pz.Div., 4.Pz.Div., 1.Kav.Div.,
        10.Inf.Div.(mot.)
XLVII.Pz.Kp. - 17.Pz.Div., 18.Pz.Div., 29.Inf.Div.(mot.)

XLVI.Pz.Kp. - 10.Pz.Div., SS-Div.(mot.) 'Das Reich'
reserve - Inf.Rgt.(mot.) 'Großdeutschland'
Pz.Gr.3 -
XLIX.Pz.Kp. - 7.Pz.Div., 20.Pz.Div., 14.Inf.Div.(mot.),
         20.Inf.Div.(mot.)
LVII.Pz.Kp. - 12.Pz.Div., 19.Pz.Div., 18.Inf.Div.(mot.)
reserve - 'Lehr' Brig.(mot.)
Pz.Gr.4 -
XLI.Pz.Kp. - 1.Pz.Div., 6.Pz.Div., 36.Inf.Div.(mot.)
LVI Pz.Kp. - 8.Pz.Div., 3.Inf.Div.(mot.)
reserve - SS-Div.(mot.) 'Totenkopf'

This was a powerful army, but it was far from satisfactory compared with the Soviet forces. However, much to the surprise of part of the world and almost to the shock of the Soviets, the Germans overcame all their problems and smashed the Soviet border with a concentration of strength in Lithuania, western Belorussia and the Ukraine, and started an advance into Russia. The world had never before seen such large-scale armored battles as those that took place during the first Russian summer. The greatest took place in western Ukraine, where the Germans faced over 4,000 tanks, many of which were used to counterattack against von Kleist's Pz.Gr.1. The Soviets attacked with four mechanized corps beginning 26th June with such strength that the lines of Pz.Gr.1 were broken in one spot. The Soviets penetrated the German defense, which was composed of units from three infantry divisions, and the Germans suffered the loss of many vehicles. However, the staffs of XLVIII.Pz.Kp. and its 11.Panzerdivision didn't panic, but continued the attack eastward. The Germans counterattacked with their right flank and completely defeated the two strongest of the four Russian corps - 4th Mechanized Corps and 8th Mechanized Corps, whose tanks had been useless since 29th June due to a lack of fuel and then ammunition.

By the beginning of July the battle was over and the German divisions started to pursue the Soviet units in the direction of the Black Sea. Behind them they left about 2,000 knocked-out Soviet tanks and about 20 times fewer German tanks. During the first two and a half weeks of similar combat all around the western part of Soviet Union, the Red Army lost about 12,000 tanks and self-propelled guns, while divisions of the Panzerwaffe lost only a little over 300 tanks!

After the collapse of the Soviet armies concentrated in the Kiev area, the new German operation "Typhoon" started. It was aimed at Moscow, and the main assault force was, of course, made up of divisions of the Panzerwaffe. They were reinforced by two new Panzerdivisions, the 5.Pz.Div. and 2.Pz.Div., but this decision didn't help as much as was necessary. The main problem was the lack of trucks and tractors; 20-55% of these vehicles were missing in most of motorized sub-units. But during the whole of September, when Guderian and von Kleist fought against Soviet forces defending Kiev, guns and vehicles arrived from Germany to replenish the divisions of the Army Group Center. Thanks to these supplies the average percent of soft-skinned vehicles lost was decreased to about 25%.

Operation "Typhoon" started on 30th September. Its first phase ended in the middle of the October with the Soviets suffering tremendous losses. The losses incurred by the Panzerdivisions were very small, but another problem arose — the weather. Because of this new enemy divisions of the Panzerwaffe could not be used in as successful a manner as in previous months. Rains mired the roads, many of which were seriously damaged. Together with the effectiveness of special Soviet units, this stopped the German thrust. A few weeks later the German advance was finally broken.

When the frosty winter came, the Panzerdivisions began to suffer heavy losses. In December 1941 they typically had only 4,000-6,000 soldiers and 30-70 tanks, so they couldn't be used as true offensive units. They were so exhausted that when the Soviets counterattacked many of the divisions very quickly lost almost all their tanks and vehicles due to technical breakdowns and a lack of fuel. In this situation, 1941 ended on a grim note for the Panzerwaffe.

During six months of combat, the divisions and battalions of the Panzerwaffe lost about 2,600 tanks and StuGs. Many of the units were so badly battered that they needed a long rest and many fresh troops. But this does not mean that the Panzerwaffe lost this campaign, as was written in a number of sources. Just the opposite is true. The Panzerwaffe won the campaign for the German forces and proved that the "Blitzkrieg" concept was the best choice for the modern battlefield. Thanks to the actions of the Panzerdivisions supported by the Luftwaffe, the Soviets lost 20,500 tanks or self-propelled guns and 3,000 other armored vehicles. Also, the German Army was able to conquer vast areas of land in a short time. This "Blitzkrieg" duo — aircraft and armor— was also responsible for the capture of hundreds of thousands of soldiers and the destruction and capture of thousands of guns, trucks, trains and other military objectives.

The Second Summer - 1942

The Germans were prepared as well as possible for the summer of 1942. During the first four months of that year, the Wehrmacht high command formed new divisions, replenished all other units and supplied them with new weapons. Based on lessons learned from Operation

"Barbarossa", the Germans started developing new types of tanks and support vehicles, many of which were able to be put into service at the end of the year. However, during the Panzerwaffe's preparation for the second round, many problems arose in relation to the armament of units. In January 1942, the German industry produced the first 64 Pz.Kpfw. IIIs which featured the new, more powerful 5cm guns. In April, production began on the first 80 Pz.Kpfw. IV Ausf. F2s, which were armed with the 7.5cm KwK40 L/43 gun, and 36 StuG III Ausf. Fs, which were equipped with the same gun. Production of these vehicles, which were the two most important assets of the Panzerwaffe, was slow, however. Up to the winter of 1942 only 70-90 pieces of each had been produced monthly. Throughout 1942, the Pz.Kpfw. III and Pz.Kpfw. IV remained the main tank used in the Panzerdivisions.

The problems related to the production of the Sd.Kfz. 251 half-track were not much easier to resolve. Twelve hundred of these vehicles were produced in 1942, which was four times more than in the previous year. However, up to the time of the summer offensive, the supplying of this particular vehicle to the infantry battalions of the rapid attack forces had been sporadic. The German Army high command could only concentrate 1,495 tanks out of a grand total of 5,385 tanks (including 264 command tanks) for Operation "Blau". As of 1st June 1942, there were 2,306 Pz.Kpfw. IIIs and only 681 Pz.Kpfw. IV tanks at the disposal of the Panzerwaffe. Interestingly, only 3,251 of these tanks were classified as being front line quality, so the Germans had to use fewer tanks for Operation "Blau" than in the previous year!

This weakness was intensified by the branch of industry responsible for the production of ammunition. Each crew of the long-barreled 7.5cm gun had only 110 shells on the average, 40 of which were armor-piercing Pz.Gr.40 shells, and they could not bank on greater supplies of this round being available. Unfortunately, it was this shell that could destroy any Soviet tank at a range of 1,000 meters (1,093 yards) and provided German crews superiority over the enemy.

Things looked a little brighter, however, thanks to other armored vehicles that supported the main tank force, especially the StuG assault guns. The Germans had 697 of these vehicles on 1st June. Also, there were up to 1,000 other combat vehicles and a few hundred Sd.Kfz. 250/251s available. About 50% of the StuGs and 75-80% of the other vehicles mentioned above were concentrated for Operation "Blau". But again this was not enough since the enemy had much more armor — about 6,000 tanks (all of front-line quality), of which 2,300 were concentrated against Army Group South in the early phase of the offensive. Also, a few hundred tanks were kept in reserve by the Red Army high command.

By the beginning of July 1942, the German rapid attack forces for Operation "Blau" were structured as follows:

4.Pz.Ar. -
XXIV.Pz.Kp. - 11.Pz.Div., 9.Pz.Div., 3.Inf.Div.(mot.)
XLVIII.Pz.Kp. - 24.Pz.Div., 16.Inf.Div.(mot.),
Inf.Div. 'Großdeutschland'
6.Armee -
XXXX.Pz.Kp. - 3.Pz.Div., 23.Pz.Div., 29.Inf.Div.(mot.)
1.Pz.Ar. -
III.Pz.Kp. - 16.Pz.Div., 22.Pz.Div.
XIV.Pz.Kp. - 14.Pz.Div., 60.Inf.Div.(mot.)
17.Armee -
LVII.Pz.Kp. - 13.Pz.Div., SS-Div. 'Wiking'

The Panzerdivisions that went into action in Operation "Blau" on 28th June were used in the same way as they were during the 1941 operations. The results of their actions were the same too — tremendous losses to Soviet defense, and a swift advance deep into enemy territory. During the opening phase of the operation, the biggest tank battle was seen in the fields east of Voronezh, where a large Soviet tank force was concentrated and put into action after a German breakthrough. Hundreds of Soviet tanks struck into the left wing of 24.Pz.Div. and Inf.Div. 'Großdeutschland', but without success. Most of the Soviet armored units were almost annihilated by German anti-tank or 8.8cm guns and Luftwaffe attacks, and on 2nd July the very first German armored troops reached the Don River. During the twenty or so days of Operation "Blau", the Germans destroyed and captured 2,400 tanks and won free passage leading to the Caucasus and Stalingrad regions. The raid to the Caucasus mountains was a very simple matter, but the battle for the Don bend ended in the streets of Stalingrad, where the "Blitzkrieg" concept was buried.

The year 1942 was unlucky for the Panzerwaffe. Though the German tankers received about 1,000 tanks more than in the previous year and lost about 100 tanks less than in 1941 (2,758 pieces), the Panzerwaffe was too weak in the decisive moments. Also, it was incorrectly used and supplied. As a result, many tanks were lost without a fight, such as in the Stalingrad cauldron for example. But the worst was still to come for the Panzerwaffe.

The Third Summer - 1943

The spring of 1943 started out very well. During one of the most brilliant operations conducted by the Germans on the Eastern Front, Gen. von Manstein recaptured Kharkov. But shortly after this victory the German advance was stopped. The German Army was exhausted, and the spring thaw turned the ground to mush. Also, the Panzerwaffe was in deep depression — its front line strength on 1st April 1943 was only 2,540 tanks! In May the situation was even slightly worse; on 1st May the Germans had only 2,504 tanks. It was the lowest level of the Panzerwaffe's strength since the beginning of the war. But it wasn't the fault of the Panzerwaffe command or the consequence of losses. The reason was the introduction of a new tank, the Pz.Kpfw. V Panther, which was organized in as poor a way as possible.

During the first four months of 1943 virtually only one type of tank was built, the Pz.Kpfw. IV Ausf. G.; in March it was produced in a quantity that just barely exceeded 200 pieces. In the same period, when only 35-45 Pz.Kpfw. IIIs had been produced monthly, only about 80 Panthers were produced, but not for front-line service. Only StuGs were produced in larger and larger numbers. So, during the first four months of 1943, the progress of the Panzerwaffe was stopped and the Wehrmacht command lost very valuable time that was needed for the preparation and realization of offensive operations. Because of this situation, the summer offensive, which received the code-name "Zitadelle", was begun early in July. However, it was the worst planned German operation on the Eastern Front. To realize this offensive, the Germans concentrated the following armored units:

Heeresgruppe Mitte
9.Armee -
XLVII.Pz.Kp. - 2.Pz.Div., 4.Pz.Div., 9.Pz.Div., 20.Pz.Div.,
        s.Pz.Abt.505, StuG.Abt.245,
        StuG.Abt.904, Stu.Pz.Abt.216
XLI.Pz.Kp. - 18.Pz.Div., 10.Pz.Gr.Div., StuG.Abt.177,
        StuG.Abt.244, s.Pz.Jäg.Rgt.656
XXIII.Pz.Kp. - StuG.Abt.185, StuG.Abt.189
XLVI.Pz.Kp. - 12.Pz.Div.
XLVI.Pz.Kp. - StuG.Abt.909
2.Armee -
Pz.Jäg.Abt.202, Pz.Jäg.Abt.559, Pz.Jäg.Abt.616

Heeresgruppe Sued
1.Pz.Ar. -
XXIV.Pz.Kp. - 23.Pz.Div., 5.SS-Pz.Gr.Div. 'Wiking'
4.Pz.Ar. -
XLVIII.Pz.Kp. - 3.Pz.Div., 11.Pz.Div.,
        Pz.Gr.Div. 'Großdeutschland',
        Pz.Abt.51, Pz.Abt.52, StuG.Abt.911
II.SS-Pz.Kp. - 3.SS-Pz.Gr.Div. 'Totenkopf',
        1.SS-Pz.Gr.Div. 'LAH',
        2.SS-Pz.Gr.Div. 'Das Reich'

Ar.Abt. 'Kempf' -
III.Pz.Kp. - 6.Pz.Div., 7.Pz.Div., 19.Pz.Div., s.Pz.Abt.503,
        StuG.Abt.228, StuG.Abt.393, StuG.Abt.905

Among all these units there were 533 StuGs and 2,239 tanks. Another 600 tanks and 464 StuGs were scattered along other sectors of the Eastern Front. Among them were 41 Flammpanzers and 67 observation tanks for artillery. Out of the mass of these tanks were 384 old vehicles (Pz.Kpfw. II, Pz.Kpfw. III and Pz.Kpfw. IV with short-barreled gun). On the other hand, there were also 178 Tigers, about 500 Panthers and 90 Elefants, which inflicted heavy losses on the Soviet Army.

The best equipped troops belonged to the Pz.Gr.Div. 'Großdeutschland' (35 StuGs and 175 tanks, including 14 Tigers and 32 Panthers) and the Waffen-SS divisions (averaging 140 tanks and 35 StuGs), which fielded almost exclusively the newest models of tanks (Pz.Kpfw. V and Pz.Kpfw. IV with long-barreled gun and side skirts). The "normal" Heer divisions had an average of about 100 tanks, but usually 40% of them were old models. So we see that the strength of the Panzerwaffe units concentrated at the Kursk bulge was the greatest of the whole war on the Eastern Front. However, due to the greater number of Soviet tanks and the greater prospects for regeneration of the Red Army troops, as well as the character of the battle itself, this armored fist was not put to productive use.

Operation "Zitadelle" was in some ways similar to World War One's Battle of Verdun. The primary goal was not the conquest of territory to set the stage for subsequent maneuvers, which would aid in completely destroying the enemy's forces. The goal was to annihilate as many Soviet soldiers and their weapons as possible during frenzied combat. This aim was achieved, but at a very high cost, of course. During the fighting in July, Germany lost 645 tanks and 207 assault guns. This was one of the greatest loss ratios suffered by the Panzerwaffe during the war against the Red Army. Although the Germans inflicted heavy losses on the Soviets, yet the Soviet factories could replace the tank losses very soon. But the destruction of the big German armored forces had a decisive impact on the outcome of the war, as Germany could never replace its tank losses at Kursk.

The tide turned for the Third Reich in Operation "Zitadelle" which marked the end of the German offensives in the East. With the Soviets mounting a counter-offensive at Orel to the north of Kursk, the Germans started to retreat by 20th July 1943.

Probably one of the best known photos showing an attack of Panzerwaffe units across open fields. Operation "Barbarossa" opened on 22nd June 1941 with a total of 3,332 German tanks involved. In the foreground is a Sd.Kfz. 253 armored command vehicle, which originally was built for StuG.Abt. (assault gun unit) staffs. Here we see this vehicle as a leading command post of a tank unit composed of Pz.Kpfw. IIs and IIIs and supported by infantry hidden in their Sd.Kfz. 251s.

This command version of the Pz.Kpfw. III, the Pz.Bef.Wg. III, was photographed while crossing a stream. Many details of the rear of this type of tank are clearly visible in this photo, including the smoke bomb rack. The most intriguing is the unusual installation of the rack for the spare road wheels on both vehicles. The tractor seen in the background was prepared to help any tank that had problems while traversing the mud.

Columns of Pz.Kpfw. IIs and Pz.Kpfw. IIIs wait in a field for the order to attack. In the center of the photo is a Pz.Kpfw. II Ausf. C with an additional box installed on the right side of the tank. There were about 700 of these tanks in front-line units during the opening phase of the war against the Soviets. They were fast, but were not strong enough to be the standard battle tank for the Panzerabteilungen. All of the Soviet standard tanks were better armed than the Pz.Kpfw. II, though this German tank was better armored than the old Soviet vehicles.

On the outskirts of a village in the southern part of the Eastern Front during the summer of 1941, a Pz.Kpfw. III Ausf. F, probably from 9.Panzerdivision, approaches a Soviet T-28 medium tank that has been completely destroyed by an internal explosion. The battles south of Luck city were the first such destructive struggles between opposing armored forces in the history of armored warfare.

Here a Soviet tank crew rides down the road with a captured Pz.Kpfw. IV Ausf. D. Note that the two rear wheels are missing. During the battle in the Luck-Rovno-Brody region, the Germans left behind their first tanks (up to about a dozen out of a total of 24,615) and self-propelled guns (SPGs), which were later claimed as captured by the Red Army. Many of them were repaired and put into service in Soviet armored units, especially from the end of 1941 to the beginning of 1943.

Columns of combat vehicles from a division that fought in the ranks of the Panzergruppe 1, which contained a total of 750 tanks and commanded by General Ewald von Kleist, advance to Kiev. Note the interesting example of tactical markings on the turret of the first Pz.Kpfw. III at right: the first number, indicating the company, is larger than others. Note also the markings painted (and partially overpainted?) on the rear of the nearest Sd.Kfz. 251. These vehicles probably belonged to 13.Panzerdivision.

Friendly conversation between SS crew members of a Sd.Kfz. 222 and Soviet peasants. As the war progressed, the partisan movement and the German Army's subsequent anti-partisan operations radically changed such behavior on both sides.

Preparation for street fighting in a town in the western region of the Soviet Union. In the foreground is a 3.7cm PAK 36 anti-tank gun, which had already proved to be an unsatisfactory weapon during the war against France. However, due to the large numbers of Soviet tanks with thin armor, it was still useful in the early months of the war against the Red Army. Armed with this type of weapon, the gun crew could knock out BT and T-26 tanks at a range of 500 meters (546.5 yards), but there are examples of combat between these types of weapons at ranges as close as 100 meters (193 yards).

A Pz.Kpfw. IV Ausf. D engages in combat on the streets of a Russian city. At the time, this was the Panzerwaffe's most powerful tank, but there were too few of them. The Pz.Kpfw. IV was not as good as the Soviet standard medium tank, the T-34, even if most of these German tanks had almost the same thickness of front armor and a similarly effective gun as the T-34 (at short ranges only).

General Harpe's 12.Panzerdivision enters Minsk in the last days of June 1941. Note the Pz.Kpfw. IV Ausf. E at the left, which is equipped with a very rare feature on tanks of this type—the smoke dischargers typical of the Pz.Kpfw. II. The tank is also devoid of a turret basket. In its place are hanging several stick grenades. Also interesting are the markings painted on the rear of the motorcycles. Each of them carries divisional emblems (the one with the sidecar even has two) in yellow and tactical markings in white.

Pursuit of the last train to freedom. One of the coaches is already hit and is burning. A Kfz. 69 anti-tank gun tractor is visible in the foreground, indicating that the coach could have been hit by a 3.7cm shell from a PAK 36 gun.

Motorcycles from a reconnaissance unit cross a provisional bridge built for the Germans by Russian villagers. It is likely that the original bridge was broken by the BT-7 tank seen at left. Bridges — or rather the absence of them — were the most troublesome factor in modern warfare during this period in the war, but the Germans efficiently overcame these difficulties during Operation "Barbarossa".

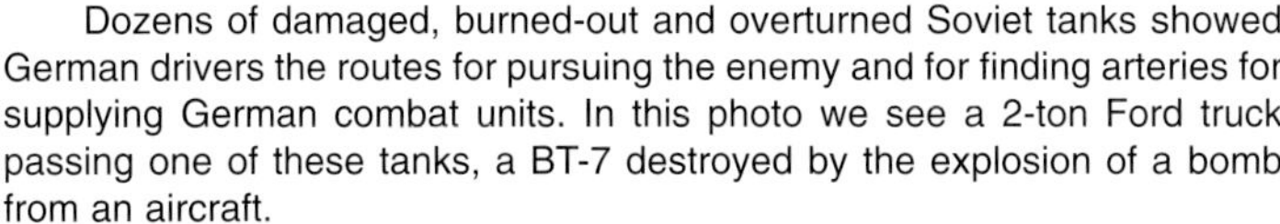

Dozens of damaged, burned-out and overturned Soviet tanks showed German drivers the routes for pursuing the enemy and for finding arteries for supplying German combat units. In this photo we see a 2-ton Ford truck passing one of these tanks, a BT-7 destroyed by the explosion of a bomb from an aircraft.

A gun duel in a local village with the soldiers accessing the damage across the road. The StuG III in this photo is marked with two concentric circles (just behind the soldier at the left), which probably indicates its company in an Abteilung.

A StuG III Ausf. B with a pair of the crew members photographed at their rest position somewhere in the western part of the Soviet Union. Judging by the heap of empty food tins behind the StuG, the crew has been there for quite some time. Note the small two-digit number, which was quite common in StuG units in 1941. The whole vehicle is painted and marked in a typical manner: dark gray camouflage and white markings. It appears that among the StuG's standard equipment were . . . slippers, which can seen on the feet of the man at left.

Here another StuG III, this time probably from StuG.Abt.244, negotiates a steep, muddy slope. Many details of the StuG III Ausf. D's upper surfaces are visible. On the mudguards we can see road markings and the emblem of the unit. The covers for the lights on the mudguards are typical of this model of StuG.

One of the main problems in the rear areas was columns of horses belonging to the infantry divisions, which was a source of many headaches for the motorized units. Here we have an example of such a situation creating a gap between the fast-moving motorized divisions of the Panzerwaffe and the infantry divisions.

A Sd.Kfz. 10 with a 5cm PAK 38 gun in tow travels down a sandy road somewhere in southern Russia. This vehicle and its gun made up the best team the Panzerwaffe possessed to fight against tanks in the early part of "Barbarossa". The vehicle was fast and mobile, and the gun was easy to handle and quite powerful. However, crews using the Pz.Gr.40 shells could fight against KV-1 tanks, too, but they had to have strong nerves since they had to let these tanks approach to within the 150-200 meter range of the gun. Note the strange wheel hub on the PAK.

Here the crew of a 5cm PAK 38 anti-tank gun from 29.Inf.Div.(mot.) is seen in successful action somewhere in Belorussia in the summer of 1941. There are three or four tanks burning in the background, with a T-34 at left, very close to the gun position. This gun, along with the Pz.Gr.40 shells, was an effective weapon against this type of tank at a range of up to 500 meters (546.5 yards).

A motorcyclist passes the burning wreckage of a Russian BT-7 tank. Visible on the rear of the sidecar is the tactical marking of the 9th company of a motorized infantry regiment. The German Army's corps of motorcycles and sidecars provided efficient assistance to the Panzertruppe.

Almost every town along the route of the German advance whose inhabitants put up any notable defense was destroyed by the Luftwaffe and artillery to prevent the German forces from suffering heavy losses. Here we can see an example of such a town being passed by German motorized and horse-drawn columns. The former, which belonged to the motorized and armored divisions, were fast, while the latter were slow. This difference in speed between the two types of columns created delays in the German advance, sometimes even creating quite large gaps in the advancing lines. Fortunately for the Germans, the Soviets were not able to avail themselves of these opportunities. The motorcycle in the foreground of the photo was produced by BMW; the second was made by Zündapp.

This Pz.Kpfw. III Ausf. F tank is loaded down with infantry troops who are being transported to battle to perform the close support needed by the tank sub-units after breaking through the front lines. This sort of troop transport was unsafe, but due to the lack of Sd.Kfz. 251s, it was the only solution. The same sort of cooperation between infantry and armored units was later used by the Soviets (who often claimed that this cooperation was their idea and was very successful) and, later, even by the Americans in western Europe.

This photo shows an attack on a lonely strongpoint where Soviet troops are positioned among farm buildings in a *kolkhoz*. Some places like this had been prepared by the Soviets for partisan operations in the 1930s, so they were well equipped with light armament and ammunition. However, many of them had already been lost in the summer due to confusion and the lack of competence of the local communist leaders, who entered into combat prematurely.

This shot shows the same action as the above photo, but it was taken a few moments later. Smoke and dust are being thrown up in a cloud after a different StuG fires a shell at a target. Note the letter "D" on the rear of the StuG's superstructure.

The advance of a heavy howitzer battery (15cm s.FH 18) being towed by horses — probably the biggest anachronism in such a modern army as the *Heer* in the era of the 1930s/40s, even more so when the horses towed artillery pieces in units which were sometimes incorporated into the Panzerkorps. At left, a Sd.Kfz. 251 Ausf. B is visible, most probably in the 251/8 version, which was for ambulance duties. The Ausf. B model was produced up to 1940, but the last of them were still in front-line service on the Eastern Front four years later.

Another type of heavy artillery, a 15cm gun, this time with a much more powerful "team", the 8-ton Sd.Kfz. 7 tractor. This photo clearly illustrates the dimensions of this type of weapon. Note the tactical marking on the vehicle.

The Germans used five main types of half-tracked tractors for their artillery units. Among them was the 8-ton Sd.Kfz. 7, visible in this photo during a trip to town to obtain supplies. This is the KMm9 version. Note how low the engine is installed. Also of interest is the license plate fixed to the rear of the side of the vehicle.

A tank unit transports stormtroopers through the German front lines during an advance against the enemy. In the foreground are two Pz.Kpfw. 38(t)s. In the background are: a PAK 38, a Sd.Kfz. 253 and a Pz.Kpfw. III. Note that the rear section of the Pz.Kpfw. 38(t) at left is completely covered by mud and dust; there is not even one small spot of dark gray visible.

A column of wheeled vehicles from a Panzerdivision belonging to General Heinz Guderian's Panzergruppe 2 move through a war-ravaged town. Panzergruppe 2 consisted of three panzerkorps totaling some 930 tanks. All of the vehicles have white road markings, which are needed for quick identification at night.

A pair of Pz.Kpfw. IIs rumble across a pontoon bridge that spans the Dnieper River. They were photographed in August 1941 as elements of Field Marshal Gerd von Rundstedt's Army Group South advanced against the Soviets into the Ukraine area. Army Group South comprised of five panzer, three motorized and thirty-four infantry divisions, plus Romanian formations.

Another river crossing by a Pz.Kpfw. II tank, this time in the far northern part of the Eastern Front, where a German tank battalion supported Finnish troops in their fight against the Soviets in the Karelian forests.

Sometimes pontoon bridges could not be used due to a lack of time or equipment, so dozens of improvised bridges were built. Here is an example of such a bridge (which was constructed by the Soviets for their motorized division) being put to good use by a German unit. Wrecks of vehicles from a Soviet unit may be seen all around this bridge and in the river. Note the fenders of the German truck — on the left one is painted the emblem of the unit, and on the right is a tactical marking.

A Pz.Kpfw. III at rest near a hut in Russia. The early Pz.Kpfw. IIIs, with their 3.7cm gun, proved to be inadequate for combat in the early 1940s, even if they were easy to operate and offered good mobility. This type of tank is an excellent example of a "half-way" weapon — much better than light tanks, but not enough good as a medium-size tank.

A motorcyclist from a reconnaissance unit observes the results of an air attack that was provided courtesy of the Luftwaffe. Soldiers belonging to these units often found themselves dozens of kilometers ahead of the closest combat units in their divisions. Note the two hand grenades just behind the headlight of this BMW motorcycle.

The armored spearhead of a Panzerwaffe unit enters yet another town wiped out by German bombardment. The Pz.Kpfw. III seen in this photo has the tactical number "525" painted on the rear of the superstructure and on three sides of the turret. The number on the superstructure is small and white, but those on the turret are large and painted in black with a white outline.

A StuG III in action. This type of armored vehicle was not armed with machine guns, so it had to rely heavily on close cooperation with ground troops. Note the tactical number and unit emblem on the cover of the smoke candle dischargers. Mud has made the emblem difficult to see clearly, though.

Another pair of StuG IIIs in action. The StuG at the left has just fired its gun, and kicked up a cloud of dust in the process. Notice the markings painted on this StuG. The tactical number is seen at the rear of the vehicle, just to the left of the national cross; the road markings are visible on the mudguard; and there is probably a unit emblem near the cross on the side of the superstructure.

This specially prepared Horch communication vehicle carries a full load of special equipment, and a squad of troops who are clearly happy to have the chance to hitch a ride. As this photo illustrates, these specialized vehicles were quite useful for transporting soldiers from one point of battle to another.

This photo, which was probably taken at a repair depot, shows an interesting meeting of vehicles from the various Panzerwaffe units. At left is a Pz.Kpfw. 38(t), at center is a StuG III, and at right is a captured Soviet T-26 light tank. Note the white national cross just visible on the turret of this tank.

Undoubtedly the greatest "hit" of the first Russian campaign were the Soviet heavy tanks of the KV-family, especially the artillery tank — the KV-2. Here we can see one of the few KV-2s captured by the Germans being presented to the public on the streets of an unknown city in Germany.

Another KV tank, this time a KV-1, is towed by two different Soviet tractors across the market square of a Russian town. The tank shows many signs of combat experience — the entire right mudguard is missing and there is a hole near the barrel of the gun.

Among the reinforcements on their way to the front lines is this StuG III Ausf. E, the newest model assault gun, which went into production in September 1941. The main difference between the "D" and "E" versions — besides a few changes in the shape of the superstructure — was the thickness of armor of the side panniers.

Troops and vehicles are shown here on their way to support the front-line units. The earlier version of the StuG III, the Ausf D, is shown here. The youthful German soldiers at left do not seem bothered by the bullet-riddled walls of the building behind them.

Supplies for the next phase of the operation arrive. Here two 7.5cm PAK 40 guns are unloaded from a train on a September day in 1941. A bigger problem than the shortage of anti-tank guns was the loss of motorized equipment, which the Germans suffered during the previous battles. There was up to a 50% rate of loss among trucks in some units.

A motorcyclist in full cold-weather dress, which even includes a protective bonnet for his helmet. The Germans learned quickly that this sort of uniform, though very useful in winter weather during peacetime and in campaigns fought in warmer months, was inadequate for the bitter Russian winter.

The main support units for the October offensive against Moscow (Operation "Typhoon") were two new divisions from the OKW reserve, the 2. and 5.Panzerdivisions, which were originally prepared for action in Africa, but were sent to Russia in September 1941. Here we see three Pz.Kpfw. IIs, five Pz.Kpfw. IIIs and three Pz.Kpfw. IVs from one of these divisions. Most of them are painted in a very light paint scheme — the dark sand color that was applied to help them blend in with the North African landscape.

Tanks and staff cars belonging to Pz.Rgt.25 of 7.Panzerdivision are seen here during their advance against the Soviet positions in the Vyazma pocket in early October 1941. It was probably the Panzerwaffe's least costly and easiest battle during that year. Panzerdivisions lost only about 100 tanks, but completely decimated Soviet defensive lines while cutting off 600,000 enemy soldiers and thousands of heavy weapons and vehicles.

A lone Sd.Kfz. 261 light armored radio car passes by a destroyed industrial building in a town somewhere on the road to Moscow. The first half of the distance to Moscow was covered by the Panzerwaffe troops without excessive difficulty. The Sd.Kfz. 261s were issued to the signal troops of the headquarter units.

A council of war between soldiers belonging to a spearhead unit and members of the staff of the unit. The tactical marking of signal troops is clearly visible on the left fender of the car. The variety in uniforms seen here is noteworthy.

One of the most difficult activities undertaken by the Panzerwaffe units was crossing a river without the help of any bridge and when the river bottom created problems. Suffering most in these situations were soft-skinned vehicles, which were unprepared for such duty. Many of them stalled in the river due to water penetrating the engine compartment.

The result of the snow and rain that fell during the first half of October was the so-called muddy season, when nearly every road disappeared for a few weeks. The soft, or more correctly liquid terrain stopped German armor cold and helped the Soviets to prepare for the defense of Moscow.

This photo shows the reloading of Pz.Kpfw. 38(t)s that have bundles of wood attached to their turrets and the front of their hulls. Petrol cans and boxes were stored at the rear of the turret. Such heavily equipped turrets were not commonly seen in units armed with these tanks, and such sights were probably limited to October 1941. The first wet snow fell on 5th October. During the next few days combat conditions changed very much.

A typical picture of combat action in the late autumn of 1941. The main road in this village looks more like a lazy stream than solid ground. The StuG III seen here belongs to StuG.Abt.192, which used the "Totenkopf" (Death's Head) as its emblem (it is barely visible on the left front of the superstructure below the tactical number "24"). There was only a small area of original color visible on vehicles used during such periods, usually in the spots that were high and were not used by crews. Therefore, the correct color of almost the entire vehicle should be dirty gray-brown — dark when fresh and wet, but light when dry.

Armored warfare on the Eastern Front was sometimes very determined, and when ammunition ran out, the Soviet and German crews did not hesitate to ram their tanks against enemy combat vehicles. This photo is a record of such extreme combat measures.

An example of the result of a StuG III ramming a T-34 is shown here. Note that the German soldiers did not even wait for the Russian crew to evacuate their T-34 before starting to look for something interesting in the Soviet tank's boxes. The crew of this T-34 was later taken prisoner.

A soldier and a StuG III— two inseparable elements during almost every action on the Eastern Front throughout the war. Note the paint job on the assault gun; white paint has been applied to all the places that were easily accessible between the wheels and the construction and to the hull and superstructure sides.

A close-up of a StuG III hiding in a wintry forest while its crew waits to go into action. The strength of the StuGs increased during the second half of 1941. The losses were low (19-22 per month maximum), so normal production could cover all of them. As of 1st December there were 598 StuGs in the Panzerwaffe — the highest level for the whole year (on 1st January there were 184 vehicles).

`Quite an unusual sight — a half-track tractor, the Sd.Kfz. 7, uses some railroad tracks to tow a damaged StuG III mounted on a railroad flatcar. Note the markings on the side of the superstructure — a circle and probably the letter "F" painted in white (part of it is visible to the right of the cross). Between them, partly covered by snow, is the national cross.

Repairing damaged parts on tanks during the winter of 1941/42 was one of the hardest duties for the Panzerwaffe crews. Here two tankers dressed in typical clothes for the season struggle with numb hands to repair the chassis of a Pz.Kpfw. IV. The Germans advanced to the suburbs of Moscow end November 1941, but it was the closest they could get. Soviet reinforcements bolstered the defenses and with inadequate clothing and equipment for the Russian winter, the Germans failed to take Moscow. General Zhukov's counter-offensive in December pushed back the Germans over 50 miles, saving Moscow.

A German soldier waits patiently for the enemy at his battle station. Sd.Kfz. 10/4s were armed with 2cm Flak 38 guns and very often were partially armored, especially for land combat. Here we see an example of such a vehicle equipped with frontal armor for the engine and an armored cab. Note the tactical marking on the right fender.

Here we see the results of the Soviet counter-offensive in the Moscow area — a dumping ground of tanks that used to belong to the Panzerdivisions. Among the six damaged tanks visible in this photo are two Pz.Kpfw. IVs and four Pz.Kpfw. IIIs. Many of the repair depots like this one were abandoned due to the loss of terrain to the enemy.

Wide, endless fields of wintertime Russia as viewed from the turret of a Sd.Kfz. 222 light armored car. Note the details of the gun (2cm KwK38 and MG34) installations. The net in the turret top cover is partly eliminated for better visibility.

Another Sd.Kfz. 10/4 half-track photographed during the winter of 1941/42 while crossing a snow-covered field. Note the unit emblem painted on the side of the combat compartment. Modelers will benefit from observing the way the snow clings to the various parts of the vehicles.

The Germans had many problems with camouflaging their tanks for winter operations at the beginning of the first winter season, and it was not until the end of the year that they started to use white paint or whitewash. Here is an example of an interesting winter pattern worn by a Pz.Kpfw. III Ausf. H. Both Pz.Kpfw. IIIs visible on this rail transport belonged to a staff unit, and both of them have pennants.

In this photo we see a Pz.Kpfw. III camouflaged with a solid coat of white paint, but behind this tank is a Pz.Kpfw. 38(t) without any winter camouflage. Note that even the tracks fixed to the hull of the Pz.Kpfw. III are painted white.

This combat photograph shows brothers-in-arms — a German tank offering a ride to Finnish troops — in action in the far north of the Eastern Front. They are pursuing retreating Soviets to the Murmansk-Moscow railroad. Murmansk was an all-weather port surrounded by a tundra belt.

A Pz.Kpfw. 38(t) advances toward a distant power station somewhere in Russia. During combat in December 1941, the Panzerwaffe units lost 102 of this type of tank out of the 434 that it possessed on the first day of that month.

Tank crew taking a break from the action in the outskirts of a forest following an exhausting series of fights during a long retreat. Note that the tank has its winter camouflage (most probably painted with whitewash) almost completely washed away. Note the improvised funnel for warming use.

Along with some ground troops and other vehicles of 6.Panzerdivision, a Pz.Kpfw. II approaches the outskirts of a Russian village. The tank is still not covered with white camouflage, but the soldiers wear the white combat smocks that we know as the typical uniform for the winter season 1941/42.

Here we see more of the offensive involving German and Finnish cooperation. The Pz.Kpfw. III has the tactical number "332" painted in yellow on all three sides of the turret. The tank is also missing most of its mudguard.

The Soviet offensive all along the front stretching from Leningrad to the Black Sea was initiated in January 1942. The Germans fought with desperation with the Soviets not gaining too much ground. But the fighting went on up until April. Here we see German troops supported by a Pz.Kpfw. III, which is still covered with solid coat of white paint, even though the weather has already turned warm.

During preparations for a new offensive in May 1942, Field Marshal von Bock visited the Panzerdivision commanded by Maj.Gen. von Apell. Here we can see von Bock visiting one of his best crews. His tank, the new model of the Pz.Kpfw. IV, the Ausf. F2, is seen in the background. It is armed with a new gun, the long-barreled 7.5cm KwK40 L/43. Von Apell's 22.Panzerdivision won fame during the fighting on Kerch Peninsula in the spring of 1942.

A photograph of a Flammpanzer B-2(f) built on the chassis of a captured French Char B-1 bis medium tank in 1941 and used by s.Pz.Kp.223 during the summer fighting in 1942 in the Crimea. There were twelve of them used in that combat. Note that the tank still lacks tactical markings.

Another view of the former French Char B-1 tank, now in service with the German Army as a Flammpanzer B-2(f). It now bears a white tactical number "114" on the turret, a national cross and a strange letter "S" on the side of the chassis.

This photo shows a lengthy procession of German vehicles loaded with press reporters during movement across the captured Kerch region in the Crimea in June 1942. Note the French Citroen half-track at the right of the photo.

15cm sIG33(Sf) auf Panzerkampfwagen I Ausf. B, 10.Panzerdivision, Operation "Barbarossa", summer 1941

This self-propelled gun had the turret and superstructure removed from the Pz.Kpfw. I Ausf. B and replaced by a large gun shield with open top and rear. The 15cm sIG heavy infantry gun on its carriage was mounted in this enclosure. This vehicle was attached to 10.Panzerdivision throughout the whole "Barbarossa" campaign. It was painted dark gray overall, with the gun shield marked with the national cross. Unit markings composed of the number of the sIG company ("706" in white) and divisional sign in yellow.

Pz.Kpfw. IV Ausf. E, regimental staff vehicle, unknown division, western Soviet Union, summer 1941

Some divisions used a marking system for their regimental staff vehicle other than the R designators. In this case it is represented by the number "901" which was the vehicle used by the commander. The tank is painted in dark gray, the typical color for this period of time. The Ausf. E was armed with a 7.5cm KwK37 L/24 gun and was one of the main battle tanks used in Operation "Barbarossa" in June 1941.

Pz.Kpfw. 38(t) Ausf. E/F, 7.Kompanie, Pz.Rgt.204, 22.Panzerdivision, Crimea, May-June 1942

The 22.Panzerdivision was one of the nine Panzerdivisions that were concentrated under Heeresgruppe Sued in preparation for the summer offensives - Operation "Blau". This tank has the standard dark gray color, but is supplemented with an irregular pattern of dark yellow color. The Nazi flag was used for air identification purposes, and is seen here affixed to the engine deck.

7.62cm PAK 36(r) auf Fahrgestell Pz.Kpfw. II Ausf. D, 3.Inf.Div.(mot.), Kalatch, November 1942

By mounting the captured Soviet 76.2mm anti-tank gun on the Pz.Kpfw. II Ausf. D chassis, the end result was the Sd.Kfz. 132. These self-propelled anti-tank gun were issued to the Pz.Jäg.Abt. (Sf) of the Panzer and Panzergrenadier divisions in 1942, and mainly used on the Eastern Front. This vehicle wasn't prepared for the winter and carried the standard dark gray paint. The two digit tactical number indicates the vehicle belonged to a self-propelled anti-tank company of the anti-tank battalion. Note the four kill rings on the barrel.

Sd.Kfz. 10/5, 2cm Flak 38 auf Fahrgestell Zugkraftwagen 1t, 7.Panzerdivision, Eastern Front, winter 1942/43
A 2cm Flak 38 anti-aircraft gun mounted on the 1t Demag D7, this Sd.Kfz. 10/5 was assigned to an anti-aircraft unit of the 7.Panzerdivision. It carries a typical winter camouflage composed of an irregular coat of white paint applied with a brush all over the vehicle. An armored cab was provided as well as an armored shield fitted to the 2cm Flak gun.

Pz.Kpfw. VI Ausf. E Tiger, s.Pz.Abt.502, Leningrad sector, winter 1942/43
This Tiger, one of the few that were hastily sent to the Leningrad sector, carries a white camouflage scheme over the dark gray overall in the winter of 1942/43. The three digit number followed the standard system. Many vehicles of the same unit didn't carry any markings once the whitewash been applied.

Sd.Kfz. 251/9 Ausf. C, 19.Panzerdivision, III.Pz.Kp., Belgorod, July 1943
This vehicle belonged to one of the armored battalions of a Panzergrenadier regiment of 19.Panzerdivision that operated near Belgorod during Operation "Zitadelle", as part of Army Detachment "Kemp". It is painted in a type of camouflage that was most probably ordered by the division command. Quite typical of German armored divisions during this period, it is composed of dark green spots outlined with brown over a standard dark yellow background.

Sd.Kfz. 250/9, Aufkl.Abt. of 19.Panzerdivision, Belgorod, July 1943
This Sd.Kfz. 250/9 reconnaissance half-track armed with a 2cm gun served with the Aufklärungbataillon of 19.Panzerdivision. The vehicle wears the same type of camouflage as the Sd.Kfz. 251/19 shown above and carries the black and white tactical number "213", which indicates it is the 3rd vehicle in 1st platoon of 2nd company.

Sd.Kfz. 231 schwere Panzerspähwagen 8-Rad, Pz.Gr.Div. "Großdeutschland", Kharkov, February-March 1943

Employed in the reconnaissance role, the Sd.Kfz. 231 8-wheeler were issued to the heavy platoon of the Panzerspähwagen squadron of each motorized Aufklärungs detachment. This vehicle carries a winter whitewash over the dark gray, with tactical markings painted over, which blended in well with the Russian winter.

Pz.Kpfw. IV Ausf. H, 1.SS-Panzergrenadierdivision "Leibstandarte Adolf Hitler", Prokhorovka, southern sector of the Kursk bulge, July 1943

The battle of Prokhorovka was the greatest armored confrontation in history. The II.SS-Pz.Kp. deployed approximately 600 tanks and assault guns against the Soviets. The Pz.Kpfw. IVs of the 1.SS-Pz.Gr.Div. were used in the flank supporting the Tigers. This vehicle is camouflaged with a green pattern on a dark yellow background. The tactical number "546" was painted in an enormous size and shape.

Pz.Kpfw. IV Ausf. H, Pz.Rgt.3, 2.Panzerdivison, XLVII.Pz.Kp., northern sector of the Kursk bulge, July 1943.
The white tactical number "631" was painted only on the rear of the turret skirt. The digit "6" is separated from the two others by the partition line of the skirt. The divisional emblem, a yellow trident, was painted on the left side of the superstructure rear plate, near the national cross. On the bin was painted a white circle with a black swastika for air identification.

Pz.Kpfw. V Ausf. D Panther, Pz.Abt.52, Pz.Rgt.39, 10.Panzerbrigade, southern sector of Kursk bulge, July 1943
This Panther Ausf. D belonged to the 1.Kompanie of Pz.Abt.52, Pz.Rgt.39. The regiment had around 200 Panthers at the start of Operation "Zitadelle" and was attached to Pz.Gr.Div. "Großdeutschland". This early production vehicle had no side skirt fitted. The tank has a color scheme of dark yellow oversprayed with green and carries a white unit emblem - the roaring panther head.

Sturmgeschütz mit 8.8cm PAK 43/2 Elefant, Pz.Jäg.Abt.654, Kursk bulge, July 1943

The Elefants were issued to Pz.Jäg.Abt.653 and 654 in the spring of 1943, and took part in the battle of Kursk. There were 45 Elefants in Pz.Jäg.Abt.654 in the Kursk offensive, and the battalion was part of Pz.Jäg.Rgt.656 attached to 9.Armee. The Elefant was an effective tank destroyer at long range. This early production vehicle was used by the staff unit of the battalion, as indicated by the white "II02". It has a dark yellow and olive green camouflage.

Sturmpanzer IV Brummbär, Stu.Pz.Abt.216, 21.Pz.Brig., Kursk bulge, July 1943

There were 66 Brummbärs in Stu.Pz.Abt.216 that took part in the battle of Kursk. Armed with the 5cm StuH43 L/2 gun on Pz.Kpfw. IV chassis, this self-propelled assault gun was produced in 1943 in time to rush to the Eastern Front for the Kursk offensive. This vehicle carries a dark yellow color oversprayed with olive green camouflage.

Sd.Kfz. 7/2, 3.7cm Flak 36 auf Fahrgestell Zugkraftwagen 8t, unknown unit, southern sector, Eastern Front, late summer 1943

The Sd.Kfz. 7/2 was an 8-ton half-track mounted with a 3.7cm Flak 36 gun. The engine compartment and driver's cab of this vehicle was armored. The Flak 36 could be given an anti-tank capability and thus very effective against ground targets. This vehicle is painted in a three-color camouflage scheme, with green patches outlined by brown over a dark yellow base. Its engine is covered by a camouflage net.

Sturminfanteriegeschütz 33B, Pz.Rgt.201, 23.Panzerdivision, southern Russia, late summer 1943

This StuIG33B belonged to the Sturm schwere Infanteriegeschütz company that was formed as the 9.Kompanie, Pz.Rgt.201, 23.Panzerdivision in late 1942. The 23.Panzerdivision was part of the XXIV.Pz.Korps assigned to Heeresgruppe Sued during Operation "Zitadelle". The vehicle had the 15cm sIG33 gun mounted on the Pz.Kpfw. III chassis and housed by a fully enclosed fighting compartment. The vehicle wears a dark green camouflage pattern over a dark yellow background and non-standard tactical markings.

The Pz.Kpfw. IV tank was not the only armored vehicle to receive new weapons. The StuG III was rearmed with long-barreled StuK40 L/43 guns, too. The photo shows one of the very early examples of the new StuG III Ausf. F, or the so-called StuG 40, which is leading a column of StuG IIIs that are still armed with short-barreled guns. In the background is an old type of 1.5-ton truck towing a 3.7cm PAK 36 gun.

This photo clearly shows the length of the barrel of the 7.5cm PAK 40 anti-tank gun, which is crowned with an oversized muzzle brake. This gun had been the best anti-tank weapon on the Eastern Front since the middle of 1941 when it was introduced to the battlefield. It gave the Germans superiority over Soviet armor for the next two and a half years.

The assault has begun! Armored vehicles of 24.Panzerdivision are seen here during their march through the steppes of the Ukraine in the direction of Voronezh. Hitler launched Operation "Blau" on 28th June 1942 with Army Group South advanced from a front between Kursk and Karkov to take Voronezh on the Don River. In the background are Pz.Kpfw. IIs, which made up the spearhead of the division's armored fist. At left is a Pz.Kpfw. III Ausf. H. At right is a communications vehicle — the Sd.Kfz. 251/6. However, the most interesting is the vehicle in the middle of the photo. It is the Sd.Kfz. 253 armored observation post, but it is modified in a very strange way — it has an additional superstructure with a roof, which is open at the moment. All vehicles are camouflaged with a dark yellow pattern over a dark gray background, and both half-tracks are carrying numerous markings.

Another strangely modified half-track of 24.Panzerdivision photographed during the advance of divisional armor in the rear areas of the front line. There is no doubt that this is a Sd.Kfz. 250/3 communications vehicle modified by workshops of the division. It is camouflaged with a dark yellow pattern, too. Note that the national cross is somewhat overpainted by the camouflage coat.

While 24.Panzerdivision covered the left flank of its corps, the Inf.Div. "Großdeutschland" advanced toward Voronezh. In this photo we see a Sd.Kfz. 251 from this division carrying soldiers who wave a greeting to a Stuka dive bomber after its ground attack mission. The emblem of the unit and the tactical markings are faintly visible on the rear door of the combat compartment.

Apart from 24.Panzerdivision, which captured 28,000 prisoners and destroyed or captured 1,000 tanks and 500 guns while guarding the flank of XLVIII Pz.Kp., the Inf.Div. "Großdeutschland" was the most famous division — not only in 4.Pz.Ar. but within the whole *Heer*. At the time the division was under the command of Lt.Gen. Hoernlein, who we can see in this photo standing with field glasses on a command version of the Sd.Kfz. 251 Ausf. B. Note that the front of the combat compartment of this half-track is covered by an armored shield where a machine gun has been fitted for anti-aircraft duties.

This shot shows to advantage the advance of an armored unit. It is a very good example of a typical tank attack seen in the Eastern Front. In this case it is conducted by medium tanks (Pz.Kpfw. IIIs) and a few light tanks (Pz.Kpfw. IIs) in the second line.

The crew of a 5cm PAK 38 anti-tank gun from Inf.Div. "Großdeutschland" waits for the approach of the enemy. Note the hand grenade ready to use just under the gun's lock and the armor-piercing round visible in the hands of the soldier at right.

The Inf.Div. "Großdeutschland" captured a bridgehead at the Don River and entered the outskirts of Voronezh on 4th July 1942, where they met a number of counter-attacks from Soviet armor. This photo shows some T-34 tanks (of the spring series produced by Stalingrad's STZ "Barricades") and a T-60 light tank destroyed in the battle. Note the triangle unit emblem on the turret of the tank at left.

This photo illustrates the results achieved by the gunners of Inf.Div. "Großdeutschland" in action against a Soviet tank brigade. It is the same battlefield as seen in the photo of the previous page. The refuse of war seen here are T-34s and T-60 light tanks.

On a nearby street sit two T-34s and a pair of T-60s, additional victims that were knocked out by the efficient tank crews of the Inf.Div. "Großdeutschland". The physical destruction inflicted by warfare is well documented here.

A few hundred meters away from the downtown area is another battlefield where three more derelict T-34s sit as monuments to the destructive power of the German Panzerwaffe. The T-34 was a formidable weapon, but it was not equipped with a radio, which would have provided much-needed communications among the tanks.

A Pz.Kpfw. III photographed while running over Soviet field positions to help out the infantry. This type of tank was still the most popular tank of the Panzerwaffe in the middle of 1942. Each month during this period almost 250 of this tank and 150 of all other tanks were built. The strong interest in this tank shown by the leaders of the Panzerwaffe in that year was one of their biggest mistakes.

A pair of Pz.Kpfw. IV Ausf. Es seen shortly after a victorious duel with Soviet tanks after breaking through their front lines. The Pz.Kpfw. IVs with the short-barreled gun were not strong enough to fight against Russian T-34 and KV-1 tanks, so the duels between these vehicles proved dangerous for Pz.Kpfw. IV crews. After rearming the Pz.Kpfw. IV with KwK40 guns, the Germans achieved superiority over Soviet tanks.

Another group of Pz.Kpfw. IVs, this time Ausf. Ds, halt behind enemy lines to receive a message from headquarters delivered by an Fi 156 Storch. Usually the most important orders were sent by aircraft to prevent the Soviets from monitoring radio traffic.

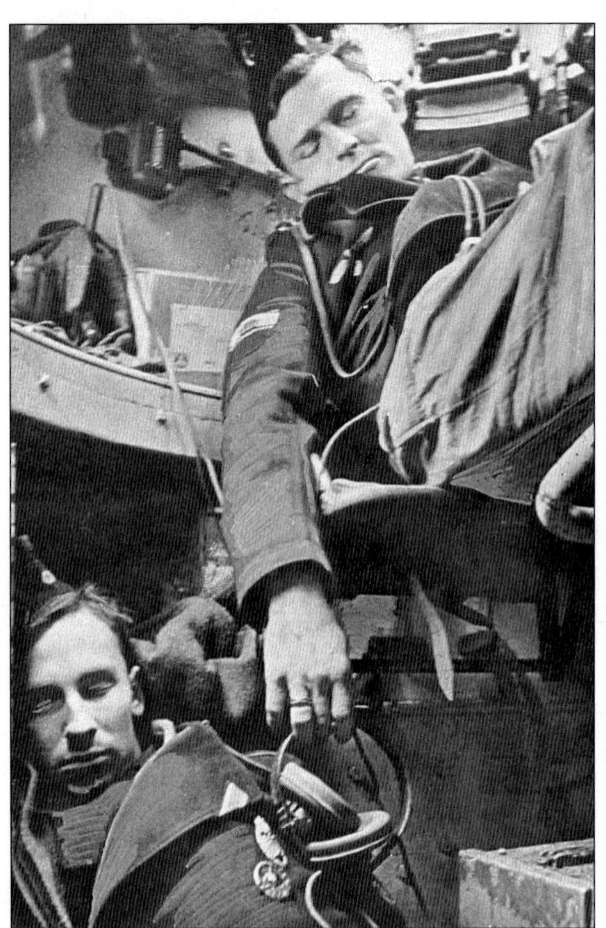

A seemingly endless train of half-tracks and trucks kicks up dust as it speeds forward to Stalingrad. This photo illustrates very well the appearance of the terrain and conditions of battles in southern Russia.

The fighting to suppress resistance in the front line area was always very hard and very exhausting, mainly due to the long duration of combat (which sometimes went on for 24 hours). Here an experienced tank crew enjoys a break in the fighting. Both soldiers are decorated with the Iron Cross First Class (EK I). One has been awarded a badge for wounds received and the other wears a patch that shows he destroyed a tank in close range combat with a grenade.

Everything could be useful in the fight against the Red Army, even their own weapons. Here is an example: an armored Komsomolets artillery tractor with a 76.2mm F-22 gun. The victory marks painted on the armored shied of the gun proves that this anti-tank crew was highly effective.

The main points of Germany's supply arteries were protected by anti-aircraft guns manned by successful crews such as this one. On the shield of this 3.7cm Flak 36 anti-aircraft gun are painted no less than 45 victory markings. All batteries were equipped with anti-tank shells, which usually were very effectively used against "Red" armor.

Another gun that the Panzerkorps put to very good use was the 8.8cm Flak 36/37 anti-aircraft gun. The one shown here installed in a cornfield belongs to a Luftwaffe unit. Note the letter "D" painted on the gun with white paint.

The same type of gun, again from a Luftwaffe unit, but this time it is ready to fight against tanks. Around the barrel are four white victory markings. Besides the PAK 40 and the Soviet ZIS-3, the "88" was the best anti-tank gun used by the Panzerwaffe.

German ground forces and armor move out en masse after receiving orders to attack new targets. At the right is a Pz.Kpfw. III with tracks hanging on the side of the turret — a sight that is not usually seen on Pz.Kpfw. III/IV tanks.

Waiting for enemy air attack. A *Luftwaffe* gun crew wearing camouflaged uniforms is ready to go into action with its 2cm Flakvierling 38 anti-aircraft gun, which is installed on a Sd.Kfz. 7 vehicle. The gun is equipped with the early version armored shield.

Quite a strange vehicle - probably a Pz.Kpfw. IV Ausf. F2 , but without the front half of the barrel and missing a machine gun in the hull position. This tank belonged to 24.Panzerdivision and was photographed somewhere in the Don River bend area in August 1942.

In the background of this scene we see a Sd.Kfz. 7 tractor towing a 15cm s.FH 18 howitzer passing a T-34 Model 42 on its way to Stalingrad. Unlike in 1941, in the period this photo was taken howitzer batteries were equipped with anti-tank shells, though in small numbers.

The Panzerwaffe's 16.Panzerdivision became its most famous division in August 1942 thanks to its great raid against Soviet positions on the Volga River, just north of Stalingrad. The sub-units of this division would hold their positions for nearly the next five months, increasing the high losses inflicted against counter-attacking Soviet divisions. In this photo the column of tanks from this division are shown on the march: Pz.Kpfw. III Ausf. Ls and Pz.Kpfw. IV Ausf. Gs. Note the non-standard exhaust system on the nearest Pz.Kpfw. IV, which is equipped with a very long exhaust pipe.

This close-up photo of a Pz.Kpfw. III Ausf. L shows very well the shape of the additional armor on the front of the turret and the length of the new 5cm KwK39 gun. The tactical number of the vehicle was censored. This model of Pz.Kpfw. III was first produced in June 1942.

The crew of a Pz.Kpfw. IV Ausf. F watches enemy movement in the dusty terrain of southern Russia in the summer of 1942. Like all other vehicles in this period, the tank was painted in standard dark gray camouflage. However, after service in such difficult country it was completely covered by a solid coat of mud and dust.

A pair of 8.8cm Flak guns are put to work firing on enemy positions at a battle position somewhere in the Caucasus area. Both guns are camouflaged with cornstalks — a standard means of camouflage due to the plenitude of cornfields in this area of Russia.

Combat along the Don River on the way to Stalingrad was not too hard on the divisions of the Panzerwaffe, mainly due to the complete surprise they achieved over the Soviet defense, which did not expect such a maneuver from 4.Pz.Armee. Here, Pz.Kpfw. III number "10" from 14.Panzerdivision is seen with other vehicles (in the background) advancing against an enemy position. Note the small division emblem on the turret just over the hatch. The length of the new 5cm KwK39 L/60 gun is clearly seen in this photo. The lack of additional armor could indicate that it is a later series Ausf. J model. Of course, it could also be an Ausf. L since not every tank with a 5cm L/60 gun was equipped with this type of armor.

From its position on the high ground, a Pz.Kpfw. III is supporting infantry troops concealed in some high grass. The tank is one of the older models, which was still standard issue in the summer of 1942.

A motorized infantry unit and its anti-tank unit, which is armed with 5cm guns, are the targets of enemy artillery somewhere in the steppes of southern Russia in the summer of 1942. The Hanomag seen in the foreground is camouflaged with a dark yellow pattern, but its insignia and markings are untouched by the paint.

Members of a Pz.Kpfw. III crew take some time out for a meal after a heated battle. Their vehicle is the standard production model seen at the end of spring and beginning of summer of 1942, either a late Ausf. J or an early Ausf. L. Note the light shade of paint on the tank. Many sources suggest that this base coat color was introduced in February 1943, but photos shows that it was already being applied in the late summer of 1942.

Crouching low in a posture typical of any soldier going into battle, a German infantryman advances through the outskirts of Stalingrad with the support of a StuG III assault gun. Vehicles of this type were indispensable throughout the entire battle in this city. The Battle of Stalingrad began on 7th September 1942, with General Friedrich Paulus' 6.Armee, with elements of the 4.Pz.Armee, attacked directly into the center of the city, with an aim to reach the west bank of the River Volga.

A tank belonging to 24.Panzerdivision passes by a trolley car somewhere in Stalingrad. Either a late Ausf. J or early Ausf. L version of the Pz.Kpfw. III, it has a special box at the rear of its hull, which was typical for this division during this period. This tank, which is camouflaged with wavy green lines, has a Nazi flag on its turret bin for air identification.

Electric trolley cars that at one time probably carried throngs of people sit empty in Stalingrad while Pz.Kpfw. III tank number "214", which is an Ausf. J, rolls by. The tank has an air recognition Nazi flag over the front of its hull to prevent attacks from friendly Luttwaffe aircraft.

One of the most successful StuG crews in Stalingrad was this one from StuG.Abt.244. During one battle in September 1942, this crew destroyed nine Soviet tanks in 20 minutes. For this achievement the commander of the crew, Oberwachtmeister Kurt Pfreundtner, was decorated with the Ritterkreuz (Knight's Cross) on 18th September (the photo shows this ceremony). The StuG III Ausf. F manned by this crew is covered with the new (at the time) dark yellow-colored base camouflage, which was introduced no later than August 1942. Note that a small part of the barrel of the vehicle, as well as its muzzle brake, are missing.

Supply vehicles of the 6.Armee in the Stalingrad area. All of them are covered with a dark yellow camouflage pattern on a dark gray background. The vehicle at left has also received a hasty application of the paint. With the Germans bogged down in the urban fighting in Stalingrad, the Soviet reinforcements closed in and eventually trapped the 6.Armee in a pocket that contained approximately 250,000 German troops. Down to some 90,000 men, Paulus finally surrendered on 31st January 1943.

This Soviet 76.2mm ZIS-3 gun that fell into German hands was photographed in its battle position. Note the non-standard shape of the gun's armored shield and the two-color camouflage. This was a powerful gun with very good tank killing capability. Needless to say it was greatly appreciated by the Germans.

A StuG III Ausf. F assault gun hides within a carefully assembled camouflaged battle station, laying in wait for an unsuspecting enemy armored vehicle to approach. There are eleven victory rings visible on the barrel of this veteran StuG.

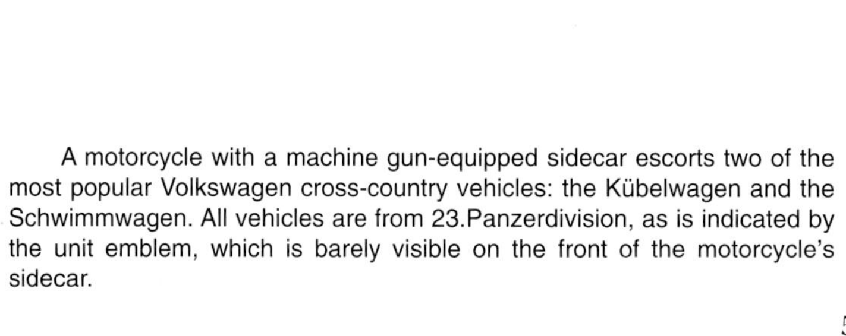

Though bundled up in warm clothing, the driver and passenger of this BMW motorcycle with sidecar no doubt yearn for spring to arrive. Note the special attention the motorcycle has received for winter survival: whitewash camouflage and snow chains on the tires.

A motorcycle with a machine gun-equipped sidecar escorts two of the most popular Volkswagen cross-country vehicles: the Kübelwagen and the Schwimmwagen. All vehicles are from 23.Panzerdivision, as is indicated by the unit emblem, which is barely visible on the front of the motorcycle's sidecar.

Under cover of an 8.8cm Flak gun (visible in the background in a specially prepared position), StuG crew members repair the damaged tracks of their vehicle. The winter camouflage on the StuG III is worn only on the superstructure and the front part of the hull. The small ring on the StuG's gun barrel is a dark gray color.

This photograph shows another battle station hiding an 8.8cm Flak 18 gun, this time from a front view. The shield of the gun is painted with an irregular pattern of white. This design would be more than adequate in such a bleak landscape.

When the 6.Armee was in peril between the Don and Volga rivers while encircled by Soviet troops on the Stalingrad Front, German troops in the central part of the Eastern Front were beating back other enemy assaults. Here are some of the soldiers that took part in that fighting. Note that the StuG III visible in the background is equipped with the so-called "Ostketten" winter tracks, even though it is the old version with a short-barreled gun.

The StuG III Ausf. G was first produced in December 1942, and the first production vehicles went into action in January of the next year. In December the production output of StuGs reached its highest level in 1942 — 120 Ausf. Fs and Ausf Gs. The losses were high, too — 40 vehicles; these were the highest monthly losses for the whole year, except in January, when the Panzerwaffe lost 53 of these vehicles.

The StuG III Ausf. G was one of the most popular combat vehicles used by the Panzerwaffe in 1943, and was effectively employed along the whole Eastern Front, from the Black Sea to the Arctic Sea. This StuG, which is named "AI", was painted very carefully with white paint and was used in the far northern part of the Eastern Front in the last days of the winter of 1942/1943.

Kettenkrads, like the one seen here, were used by many sub-units in the Panzerwaffe's light divisions. It was quite useful in Russia, especially during difficult seasons, but generally it was not a successful idea. It proved to be too small and too weak for transport duty, and too slow as a motorcycle.

A Sd.Kfz. 7/1 with an armored cab is preparing to fight from this dug-in position. Note how difficult a target the big vehicle has become when properly camouflaged with white paint and well covered by snow and frozen earth.

Here a 2cm Flak 38 mounted on a Sd.Kfz. 10/4 goes into action. This sort of vehicle was usually used as a light support weapon for infantry troops or to provide cover for armored troops. Note that the interior part of the gun's armored shield is covered with an irregular pattern of whitewash camouflage.

Dressed against the cold winter weather, a crew of an 8.8cm Flak 18 gun works their weapon during the heat of battle. Note the hastily applied winter camouflage only partially covering the gun. Of particular interest are the white markings on the gun's lock.

If the Soviet tankers were to venture close to see if there was anything dangerous in these bushes, they would be unpleasantly surprised by an anti-tank shell fired from the long, dark barrel of an 8.8cm gun. The effective camouflage covering the Flak gun was prepared not for combat, but against air identification.

The Soviet equivalent of the German 8.8cm anti-aircraft gun was the 85mm Model 39 gun. Though it was not as deadly a weapon as the German gun, it was willingly used by the German troops. They appreciated the easiness of its operation and found it more powerful than their own 5cm and 7.5cm guns. Here we see a captured full-tracked STZ-5 tractor towing an 85mm gun.

A version of a hybrid German gun, the 7.5cm PAK 97/38, which was produced by using French (Schneider Model 1897 gun) barrel and German (PAK 38) carriage parts. It had similar anti-tank capabilities as the PAK 38 with Pz.Gr.40, but was more useful as an infantry support weapon. During the winter of 1942/43, some of these guns were carried on the platforms of the Pz.Jäg.Abt. trucks, especially on the half-tracks like the Opel Maultier.

The camera has captured the precise moment when a German gunner loads a shell into the breech of a PAK 97/38 gun. Note the sharp armor-piercing tip on the shell in the hands of the loader at right. All of the gunners wear the padded uniform that was produced in the winter of 1942/43.

The Ausf. N was still a new model of the Pz.Kpfw. III in the winter of 1942/43 since its production only began in June 1942. It was armed with a short 7.5cm KwK37 L/24 gun, which had been primarily assigned to the Pz.Kpfw. IV, and which was only introduced in the Pz.Kpfw. III after the decision to rearm the Pz.Kpfw. IV with the KwK40 L/43 gun. It was one of many strange decisions common to the technocrats of the German war machine. This photo shows a tank of the earlier series without additional armor. Though the tank lacks white winter camouflage, it is equipped with "Ostketten".

The Pz.Kpfw. VI Tiger was a real shock to Soviet soldiers. Though its construction was based on an obsolete concept, the Tiger was very well armored and armed. Consequently, it very quickly dominated the battlefield. Here are vehicles from s.Pz.Abt.503, which had seen combat in southern Russia since early winter 1942/43.

Guarding the battlefield. A German patrol moves across some bleak terrain in a captured BA-64 Soviet light armored vehicle. The Germans captured perhaps ten to twelve thousand Red Army armored combat vehicles, but not many of them were used by German units as full combat vehicles. Note the prominent Nazi marking on the bow.

A close-up of a Tiger of the s.Pz.Abt.503. Visible below the barrel is the "S" anti-personnel mine discharger, which could also be used as a smoke discharger. During the initiation of the Tigers, few troubles were met. One of the main problems encountered was the Luftwaffe's lack of knowledge about the Tiger tanks. Until Luftwaffe pilots were issued special drawings of Tigers made by the staff of Army Group South, German aircraft would often attack them.

Along with some supporting infantrymen, a Tiger tank moves against an enemy position in a Russian village. Note the style of painting winter camouflage over the tank's original dark gray background — all vehicle markings are untouched by the white paint. This was quite a typical style of camouflage in the Tiger units during their first winter. The Tigers created their first serious problems for the Soviets in the northern sector of the Eastern Front, where s.Pz.Abt.502 was sent.

The end of the Panzerwaffe in the Stalingrad area. At a dumping ground somewhere on the steppes of Russia sit several Pz.Kpfw. IIIs and one Pz.Kpfw. IV with a long barrel. Note the interesting pattern of camouflage and the "K" marking on tank number "932" in the foreground. With the collapse of the German pocket at Stalingrad, the Panzerwaffe had to count all tanks of the 6.Armee - about 1,000 vehicles - as lost.

A column of Sd.Kfz. 250s with a model 250/7 armed with an 8cm mortar bringing up the rear. Each of the vehicles is equipped with folding-top tarpaulins and most probably camouflaged in the same way. The nearest Sd.Kfz. 250 is painted with a dark yellow pattern over dark gray background, and the next one received a solid coat of dark yellow paint, which completely covered the dark gray background. Note the petrol can fastened to the rear of this vehicle — it appears to be a lighter shade of paint than the color of the vehicle. Tactical markings on both vehicles (painted on the rear door) are untouched by this dark yellow paint.

This photograph is a record of the results of Tigers from s.Pz.Abt.502 going into battle near Leningrad: three destroyed BT-7 tanks and a heavily thinned-out forest. Visible at left is the rear part of Pz.Kpfw. VI. The smooth strip of land is the track of the underbelly of a Tiger tank, which was created as a result of soft ground.

Two other victims of Tigers. A pair of KV-1 tanks, which had the misfortune to be on the receiving end of 8.8cm shells, sit abandoned in a forest where the fighting has reduced the trees to toothpicks. Frenzied combat at short range in wooded areas was made even more hazardous and chaotic by fires, explosions and pieces of hundreds of falling trees.

Armored infantry is shown here attacking in the direction of Kharkov in March 1943. Note that only the Sd.Kfz. 250 visible in the middle of the photo is camouflaged. The other vehicles, Sd.Kfz. 251 half-tracks, still carry the solid white paint scheme.

A StuG III Ausf. G passing by ruins of a Soviet city at the end of winter 1943. The vehicle still exhibits the remains of winter camouflage. Note that for additional protection the crew of this StuG has affixed extra tracks to the exposed areas of the superstructure.

The main difference between the newest model of StuG III, the Ausf. G version, and the older ones was the commander's cupola, which was very helpful to StuG commanders during battle. Here we see a close-up of this modernization.

Another Panzer commander, but this one surveys the battlefield from the hull of his unidentified armored vehicle. Miniaturists will notice that for practical reasons he has removed the stiffener from the crown of his service dress cap.

During the preparation for Operation "Zitadelle" in the spring of 1943, the Germans sent a lot of armament to Russia, including many armored vehicles. This photo shows the arrival by a new rail transport of 19.Panzerdivision, which used the same divisional markings as the "Das Reich" Division of the Waffen-SS for this operation. In the photo we can see a battery composed of five StuG III Ausf. Gs from the division's StuG.Abt. Note the camouflage pattern (olive green on dark yellow background) and the emblem of the unit — the ace of spades.

An armored infantry battalion equipped with Sd.Kfz. 250s and Sd.Kfz. 251s (including the artillery model, Sd.Kfz. 251/9, armed with a 7.5cm KwK37 gun) is organized into a column at a train station. All the vehicles are painted with a special pattern of camouflage — green spots outlined with brown on a dark yellow base color. In the background are other such vehicles, as well as soft-skinned supply vehicles.

More Sd.Kfz. 251s await transport. The three-color camouflage is clearly visible on the vehicle at the far right, which is a communication version. Note that its FuG8 star antenna is installed on the right side of the vehicle and not on the left, as it usually is. Also, there is no frontal machine gun installation.

Another shot of the same unit from 19.Panzerdivision, this time presenting a close-up of a Sd.Kfz. 250/9 with the tactical number "213". The half-track is painted in the same style of camouflage on all of its surfaces. Note that even the helmet was painted with the dark yellow-colored paint by the crew.

Colonel General Hermann Hoth, wearing a Luftwaffe camouflage blouse, is talking with a soldier belonging to an anti-tank battalion from a Luftwaffe field division. During "Zitadelle" Hoth commanded the very successful 4.Pz.Armee. Note the details of the PAK 97/38 anti-tank gun visible in this photo.

Another well-known commanding officer of Operation "Zitadelle", Field Marshal Günther von Kluge, who at the time was commander of Heeresgruppe Mitte (Army Group Center). He is seen here during a demonstration of Tiger tanks in July 1943, in which he observed from his Horch staff vehicle.

During "Zitadelle" the Germans used for the first time the fully-tracked RSO tractor modified for anti-tank and artillery guns. RSOs were concentrated in independent battalions, and at the beginning of July 1943 there were four battalions that were armed with 10.5cm howitzers and towed by RSOs available in the Kursk bulge.

Though the demolition of a building is a good show of this Tiger tank's power, such action would not be practical in the heat of battle when the lives of the crew members depend on clear visibility through the visors.

Three crew members make a joint effort of cleaning a StuG III's gun barrel. This gun, a modification of the standard PAK 40, posed a dangerous threat to any Soviet tank in 1943, and even later. The Pz.Gr.40 fired from this gun could penetrate 100mm armored plating at a range of 1,000 meters (1,093 yds), so even a mighty KV-1 would be rendered helpless by such an anti-tank weapon.

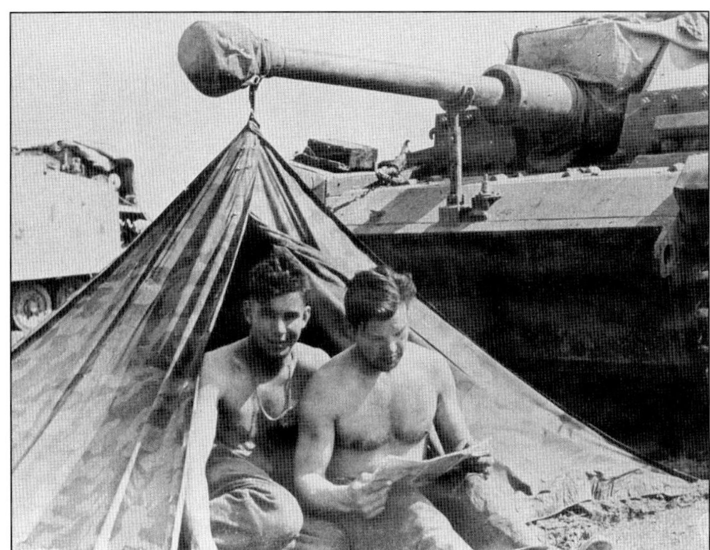

These StuG III Ausf. G crewmen have employed the strap on a muzzle brake cover to erect a shelter for themselves. There was always time for news from the Third Reich after work was complete. Note the support for the gun — a rare piece of equipment on StuGs.

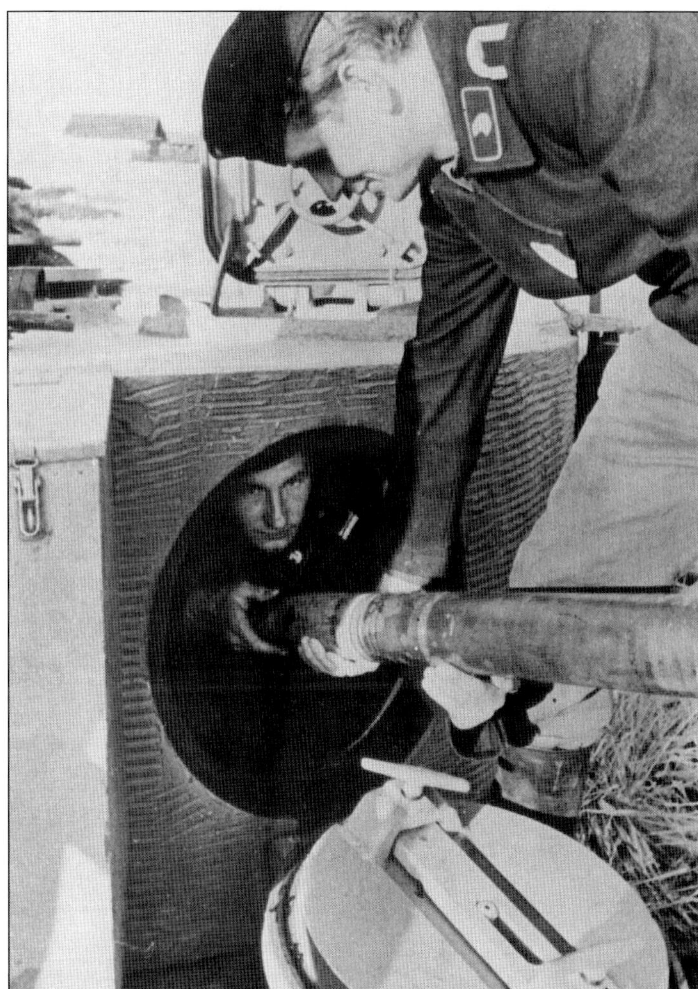

A Tiger tank crew loads ammunition into their tank through a hatch at the rear of the turret. Each anti-tank shell like this one could destroy any armored target belonging to the Red Army at a range of 1,000 meters (1,093 yds) . . . even formidable IS-2 tanks.

Having gathered their vehicles in a row, the commanders of this StuG III row receive some final orders prior to battle. Once this routine is completed, they will roll off toward the front lines. All of the StuGs are painted in the same camouflage scheme.

This photo shows the concentration area for StuG.Abt. sub-units at a position of departure near the front line. Note how the undulating terrain would protect the StuGs from view.

A few minutes later the StuGs are on their way into action. This close-up clearly shows the camouflage worn by these assault guns, which is composed of green and brown mottle irregularly sprayed over a dark yellow background.

With such a weapon as the Pz.Kpfw. VI Tiger on their side, it is no wonder that these soldiers were in such a good mood prior to Operation "Zitadelle". They no doubt felt that victory was assured. Hitler had a different opinion, however, and the German attack was stopped in the middle of July without gaining strategic success.

Roads jammed with transport vehicles were commonly seen during the last weeks before the German attack. All the vehicles in this photo — with one exception — including a Sd.Kfz. 251/7 Pionierpanzerwagen, are painted with a dark yellow-colored paint, and most of them have camouflage patterns added to this base coat.

As ground troops take up positions on the high ground, an armored battalion prepares to go into action in the fields on each side of a road. The open terrain offers the German tanks plenty of room to maneuver. The main attack force of this unit is the Pz.Kpfw. III.

Here the armored fist of 2.SS-Pz.Gr.Div. "Das Reich" is seen moving against a Soviet position. In the foreground is a Sd.Kfz. 251 painted in a two-color camouflage. Also visible are four T-34 tanks (one of them behind the Sd.Kfz. 251). Three of them are painted in a dark yellow base color with olive green and red brown camouflage, but the fourth, at right, looks darker, even if it is camouflaged with foliage. T-34s were used by Pz.Jäg.Abt. of this division.

The ability to rapidly change firing positions was one of the main factors in the success of heavy artillery. Therefore, in the beginning of 1943, the Germans began to use large numbers of self-propelled howitzers in their Panzerdivisions and korps. Here is one of the most popular types, the Hummel, which was built on a Pz.Kpfw. IV chassis and armed with a 15cm howitzer.

Another popular self-propelled howitzer was the Wespe (wasp), which was built on the chassis of a Pz.Kpfw. II and armed with a 10.5cm howitzer. Here a complete battery of these armored vehicles is seen, each one being camouflaged with green spots on a dark yellow background. All white markings are painted on the dark background of the green camouflage. A light battery was composed of six Wespes, a heavy one of four Hummels. "Zitadelle" was the first major action for the Wespe.

Operation "Zitadelle" opened on 5th July 1943. The German forces consisted of 900,000 men, 2,700 tanks and self-propelled guns, 10,000 guns and mortars, and 2,000 aircraft. Here we see Wespes at work in an open field. Note the different patterns of summer camouflage. Behind the self-propelled howitzers is an Opel Blitz truck, which is used as a supply vehicle for the battery even during combat. This truck allowed the battery to change its battle station at any given moment and not be tied to a permanent ammunition dump.

A lone Tiger holds its position in a field as it smashes Soviet resistance during the Battle of Kursk. The Pz.Kpfw. VI was the king of the battlefield during this operation. Due to the great power of their guns and excellent armor protection, Tigers were used during this operation in the front lines of the armored attack formations. They moved ahead slowly, firing on any target they saw. Just before arriving at the Soviet lines, they were overtaken by second and third waves composed of Pz.Kpfw. IIIs and Pz.Kpfw. IVs and supported by Hanomags with infantry, which then charged the enemy lines.

An armored infantry unit under enemy fire. At left a Sd.Kfz. 251/7 Pionierpanzerwagen is visible; at right is a Sd.Kfz. 250. Due to a break in war operations in the spring of 1943, few infantry battalions could be well equipped with these vehicles.

This excellent shot presents a typical picture of an armored attack during Operation "Zitadelle". In tho first line are Pz.Kpfw. IIIs armed with long-barreled 5cm guns and equipped with armor skirts (Schürzen) around their turrets. The next line consists of Pz.Kpfw. IV tanks — one of which is visible in the background.

Nothing could help in the fight against Tigers. During frontal assaults, only a lucky shot from a 76.2mm tank gun could damage a Pz.Kpfw. VI, which would have to be finished off later. Therefore, out of 33 Tigers lost during July, only about half were lost due to Soviet tank action. Here two Tigers pass by the remains of a thwarted Soviet armored counterattack.

A pair of Sd.Kfz. 250 half-tracks convey troops across a stretch of flat Russian fields as men and machines move to a concentration area prior to an upcoming offensive. These versatile vehicles could easily negotiate such open terrain.

An armored attack seen through the eyes of a Pz.Kpfw. IV radio operator from second platoon. At left are two Sd.Kfz. 251s from the second company (the first of them wears the tactical number "231"). They are equipped with spare wheels and camouflaged in strange way. In the background is a Pz.Kpfw. III.

Panzerjäger move into their firing position. This battery is equipped with Marder IIIs armed with Soviet 76.2mm guns and built on the Pz.Kpfw. 38(t) chassis. Note that a censor has blotted out the muzzle breaks. Also of special interest is the vehicle at left. Though it looks like a Marder II, it is probably a munitions vehicle built on Pz.Kpfw. II chassis.

StuG IIIs attacking enemy positions. Shown here are an Ausf. F (at left) and two Ausf. G vehicles, including one with side skirts painted with a three-color camouflage scheme. While the system of skirting was a good idea, it was not practical since individual plates were often lost before battle. The Battle of Prokhorovka marked the greatest armored clash in history, involving an estimated 1,000 tanks. Both sides suffered heavy losses. With the Allies landed in Sicily and the Soviets mounted a counter-offensive at Orel, Hitler reluctantly called off "Zitadelle" and by 20th July, the Germans were in retreat.